TAMING
TRAUMA BEASTIES:

HELPING CHILDREN CONFRONT TRAUMA AND HEAL

Front and back cover art by Zach Anderson
Cover design by Lee Clevenger
Back cover photo of Dr. Gallagher by RollsAdventure
Back cover photo of Dr. Karjala by Clayton Camera Craft
Front/back cover background photos by Gordan@fotolia.com

Choices method reprinted by permission from Patricia Carrington, Ph.D.

ISBN Number 978-0-9788571-4-1
First Printing, April 2007

Published by:

ThomasMax Publishing
P.O. Box 250054
Atlanta, GA 30325
404-794-6588
www.thomasmax.com

TAMING TRAUMA BEASTIES:

HELPING CHILDREN CONFRONT TRAUMA AND HEAL

by

Mary M. Gallagher, Ph.D.
and
Lynn Mary Karjala, Ph.D.

Illustrated by

Zach Anderson

with Dale Gettier

 ThomasMax Publishing

ACKNOWLEDGEMENTS

The authors wish to thank all the individuals who took time out of their busy schedules to review the manuscript and offer thoughtful comments. Their dedication to the welfare of children was very apparent in their enthusiastic endorsement of *Taming Trauma Beasties: Helping Children Confront Trauma and Heal.* We would like to specifically thank Terry Fishler, Jan Holbeck, Kerry Leavitt, Carla Meyer, Pam Myette, Sue Shaffer, Barbara Slater and Joyce White. Special thanks go to children Katia B., age 10, and Patrick M., age 11, for their reading and comments.

We would also like to thank the artists, Zach Anderson and Dale Gettier, for their patience in drawing and re-drawing the illustrations.

We offer overwhelming thanks and gratitude to all of the children and adult patients and their families who have shared their stories so that the Trauma Beastie concept could emerge.

Special thanks also go to Dr. Patricia Carrington for her creative ability and talents in developing the Choices method.

ABOUT THE ILLUSTRATORS

Zach Anderson lives in Roswell, Georgia, and attends Georgia State University. He is a freelance artist on the side. In addition to contributing most of the drawings for the book, Zach was responsible for bringing the Trauma Beastie to life.

Dale Gettier lives in Maryland with her husband, Ray. She is a survivor of childhood trauma and produced the drawings that depict the traditional psychotherapy interventions.

PREFACE FOR THERAPISTS, PARENTS AND CARETAKERS

The Trauma Beastie was born about 10 years ago from the work of Dr. Mary Gallagher, while she was engaged in training therapeutic foster care parents. Dr. Gallagher realized that many foster parents and case workers could not explain or identify the antecedents or triggers for an outburst of verbal or physical aggression from their foster children.

This inability to identify clear triggers led many foster parents to feel that they were poor observers or simply incompetent. Then there were many other individuals—both professionals and parents—who concluded, when they could not identify clear triggers, that the foster child was simply malicious or devoid of the capacity to have concern for others. These perceptions led to feelings of helplessness, hopelessness, and resentment and a need to blame someone for the chaos and negativity running rampant in the foster home, as well as to subtle or blatant deterioration in the family relationships. Often they also led to early burnout in the foster parents, traumatization of the foster care family and, ultimately, the uprooting and re-placement of the foster child.

It became clear that a concept was needed that could capture the pervasive and persistent negative impact of trauma without putting blame on anyone. Such a concept would give the child and those working with him or her a language that would allow them to talk about trauma-related behaviors, feelings, thoughts, and sensory experiences without triggering the child to act out these trauma symptoms. The concept of the Trauma Beastie answered this need.

Even though the Trauma Beastie was conceptualized 10 years ago, this book could not be written until now. The initial formulation of the Trauma Beastie concept could help children manage and regulate the trauma symptoms but could not neutralize them. It needed to include an intervention that could *tame* the Trauma Beastie. In 2003, Dr. Gallagher attended the annual conference of the Association of Comprehensive Energy Psychology, where she met Dr. Lynn Mary Karjala. Dr. Karjala was able to provide the missing piece, in the form of energy psychology techniques.

There are three parts in *Taming Trauma Beasties: Helping Children Confront Trauma and Heal*. The first section of the book, entitled "About Trauma Beasties," identifies the Trauma Beastie and explains key concepts about the impact of trauma. The second section, entitled "Taming Trauma Beasties," presents both traditional interventions and Choices, an energy psychology technique developed by Patricia Carrington, Ph.D. The final section is an appendix that offers additional examples of the application of Choices; a list of resources is also provided.

To review in more detail, the first section introduces the Trauma Beastie and what it embodies. Key trauma concepts are described, with drawings to help the child make a personal connection to his or her own life. As an adult reads this book with the traumatized child, additional examples can be elicited and even drawn by the child. Once the language and concepts have been mastered, they become part of the child's and adult's everyday language. For example, a five-year-old girl who had been sexually abused by her grandfather was seen in individual play therapy. The concept of the Trauma Beastie was explained to her and her parents and was introduced into the therapy. She was told in a variety of different ways that a Trauma Beastie was tricking her into believing that she was not safe when she actually was. It became clear that she had successfully integrated the Trauma Beastie concept when, one night, she came downstairs crying and stated to her parents, "The Trauma Beastie is bothering me." Even though she had not yet learned the Choices method, hugs and verbal reassurance were sufficient in this instance for the child to return to her bed and fall asleep.

Children involved in the child welfare system and, more recently, children adopted from other countries typically suffer from multiple and cumulative trauma. The devastating impact of these experiences on children's overall functioning is well documented, as is their complicated psychiatric symptomatology. This complicated pattern of symptoms is more easily understood in light of the BASK model. BASK is an acronym for the four types of components that make up our memories, both non-traumatic and traumatic. B stands for behavior, A is for affect or feelings, S is sensory (body-based processing and storage) and K is for knowledge (thoughts, beliefs and concepts). Any time a trauma is triggered, it is subtly or overtly expressed through one of these components or through a combination of several or even all components at once. For example, a twelve-year-old boy who had suffered severe physical, emotional and mental abuse as well as exposure to deadly domestic violence was playing a board game with his male therapist. Whenever the therapist got ahead of him, the boy would simply move the therapist's piece back to the beginning without a word. Despite reassurance and discussions with the boy, his behavior did not change. The therapist realized that the boy was experiencing an affective flashback. It was then pointed out to the boy that he was worried that something really, really terrible might happen when his therapist was ahead – that it somehow triggered a Trauma Beastie from his abuse. He was reminded that this was just a simple game and that he did not have to worry. The boy was then able to play the game to the end, even when it was obvious that the therapist was going to win.

The second section, "Taming Trauma Beasties," describes several techniques for dealing with traumatic symptoms. The traditional techniques are simple and self-explanatory. The first technique—stating firmly, out loud, three times that one is not going to have bad dreams—was developed by Barbara R. Slater, Ph.D. This technique is a mild form of self-hypnosis, and it has been effective for both children and adults in keeping nightmares at bay. At times, a young child may come to a session stating that his or her teddy bear or other stuffed animal is having nightmares. In such cases, the statement is said three times for the child and then three times for the teddy bear.

The drawings of putting the Trauma Beastie behind a door is meant to help children who are concrete in their thinking move to an abstract level so that they can mentally envision their containment of trauma-related thoughts, feelings and sensations. In addition, children can make stop signs and hang them in their bedrooms.

As valuable as these traditional techniques are, however, they are not sufficient to completely resolve trauma symptoms. In the example above of the boy playing a game, the verbal intervention had to be made each time he and his therapist played a game, especially the first time the therapist went ahead. In other words, the Trauma Beastie was being regulated but not neutralized. The energy psychology technique called Choices, also presented in this section, is one of the best ways the authors have found to tame Trauma Beasties. Once the Trauma Beastie is tamed, the memory loses its emotional charge, and it no longer triggers trauma-related symptoms.

The next drawings are of the children presented earlier in the book doing Choices. Choices involves tapping acupressure points. When the acupressure points are tapped, stress is released. A special *working phrase* is developed for each child. This phrase clearly reflects both the problem and the solution. It is important that children be involved in developing the working phrase. At first they will need considerable support in constructing the phrase, but with practice they will become more proficient and independent. The phrase must be constructed carefully, so that it genuinely addresses the problem at hand; for example, it will not help the child very much to tap on feeling angry if the real problem is that he or she is deeply frightened. The phrase also needs to have adjectives that stimulate excitement and draw the child in. The solution part of the phrase is always written in the present tense and in positive, engaging language, avoiding negative words such as "not."

It is important to follow the steps exactly as they are described, as well as to tap on the precise acupressure points. It is not necessary for Choices to be done during the problem situation. It can be done outside of the situation so that the child changes his or her attitude and installs a new way of thinking or solving the problem. This is important, because many children hesitate to do Choices in front of their peers. It is also important never to use Choices as a punishment—for example, when a parent tells a child who is having trouble to go to his or her room and tap, not as a positive coping strategy for the child but as an expression of the parent's own anger.

A final thought: the authors believe that early intervention with children who have suffered various forms and severity of trauma is essential. *Taming Trauma Beasties: Helping Children Confront Trauma and Heal* is written not only to intervene but to help eliminate the devastating impact of trauma at all levels of functioning.

ABOUT TRAUMA BEASTIES

Reading this book will tell you about:

TRAUMA

TRAUMA BEASTIES

FLASHBACKS

TRIGGERS

TAME

Read this book many, many times alone or with an important grownup. Your grownup will help you understand about **TRAUMA BEASTIES** and how to **TAME TRAUMA BEASTIES.**

A **TRAUMA** is something **REALLY, REALLY** scary or hurtful that happens to a person. These scary or hurtful happenings can be all kinds of things, such as not having enough food, or being hurt really badly, or having someone touch the private parts of you they're not supposed to touch in a way that makes you feel scared or very uncomfortable.

This is a **TRAUMA BEASTIE**.

A **TRAUMA BEASTIE** is made up of the thoughts, feelings, and memories of **REALLY, REALLY** hurtful and scary things that can happen to children. Many children have them. Children just like you.

Children try really hard not to let **TRAUMA BEASTIES** bother them. They watch TV, play ball, go to sleep, ride their bikes, and learn at school to help them not think about **TRAUMA BEASTIES**. Sometimes it works, and they can be happy and have fun.

But **TRAUMA BEASTIES** do bother children even when children don't want them to. **TRAUMA BEASTIES** make children feel:

SCARED,

       CONFUSED,

             CREEPY,

                   SAD,

and even **ANGRY**.

When a **TRAUMA BEASTIE** bothers children, it is called **HAVING A FLASHBACK.**

This means that children are having a memory…a remembering about their trauma…the **REALLY, REALLY** hurtful or scary thing that happened to them.

When they are **HAVING A FLASHBACK** or a trauma memory, children become CONFUSED. They think the trauma or that **REALLY, REALLY** scary time is happening right now. But it is not happening. The truth is that they are safe now.

This little girl, Sally, is happy and enjoying her bath.

But then, a **TRAUMA BEASTIE** comes and makes

her feel **SAD** and scared. She thinks her trauma or that

REALLY, REALLY scary time is happening right now!!!

She thinks her uncle is coming to touch the private parts of her he shouldn't be touching! But no one is coming. Her parents have told her uncle that he is not allowed in the house or near her anymore. She is safe now!

This boy, John, is playing tag with his best friend. He is laughing and having fun. But then, playing tag starts to feel like trying to get away from someone scary. That's a sign that a **TRAUMA BEASTIE** is there. John feels *scared*, CONFUSED and **angry**. He yells at his friend. A fight starts. Playing is no longer fun.

He thinks his mother's boyfriend is holding him down

and beating him, and he can't run away. He feels he is being

hurt!!! But it is only his friend. He is not being hurt. They

are just playing tag.

This girl, Maria, is sleeping.

But then, a **TRAUMA BEASTIE** dream happens.

She wakes up quickly. She is scared and feeling *creepy*.

She sits up and listens. She starts crying.

She thinks her trauma or that **REALLY, REALLY**

scary time is happening right now!!! She thinks her mother

and father are fighting hard.   She thinks her mother is getting

hit and … might die! But it is quiet. There is no fight.

TRAUMA BEASTIES are very tricky and clever.

They trick children into believing that the trauma or that

REALLY, REALLY scary or hurtful time is happening

right now! But the truth is that they are safe.

Nothing scary is happening.

When a **TRAUMA BEASTIE** bothers children, it is

because it has been TRIGGERED.

TRAUMA BEASTIES become

TRIGGERED whenever children are doing something that

seems like, but usually not exactly like, their trauma or that

REALLY, REALLY scary or hurtful time.

When a trauma memory is TRIGGERED, it means the memory is brought back into the child's thinking.

Children are not thinking about their trauma memory but then, all of a sudden, they are. This happens because something they were doing, listening to, smelling, touching or looking at caused their trauma or **REALLY, REALLY** scary or hurtful time to be suddenly TRIGGERED or remembered.

Remember, Sally was taking a bath. Being in the bath tub TRIGGERED the **TRAUMA BEASTIE**, because she had been in the bathtub when her uncle touched her in a way that made her feel sad and scared.

John was playing tag. When his friend held onto him, it reminded him of when his mother's boyfriend held him down and hit him, and this TRIGGERED the

TRAUMA BEASTIE.

Maria was lying in bed sleeping. Being in bed TRIGGERED the **TRAUMA BEASTIE** because

she was lying in bed when she heard her mother and father fighting.

When a **TRAUMA BEASTIE** is TRIGGERED, many children think it's their fault that the **TRAUMA BEASTIE** came. They feel that somehow they have done something wrong, and they feel bad, ashamed and even embarrassed.

But when a **TRAUMA BEASTIE** is TRIGGERED, it is never children's fault. They have done nothing wrong to cause a **TRAUMA BEASTIE** to bother them. They were only remembering.

A **TRAUMA BEASTIE** can be TRIGGERED even

when you are a grownup.

TAMING TRAUMA BEASTIES

When children have had traumas or **REALLY, REALLY** hurtful or scary things happen to them, it is important to learn about **TRAUMA BEASTIES** right away. Children then become stronger and wiser in knowing how to **TAME TRAUMA BEASTIES** and how to stop them from pestering and bothering them.

Children often do not know that they are having a memory or a **FLASHBACK.** They do not know that a **TRAUMA BEASTIE** is bothering them. They mostly have **uptight**, *creepy*, yucky, scared, **SAD,** alone or **angry** feelings.

When these feelings happen, some children yell or

scream or fight or throw things. They might break toys or

furniture or cut up clothes or schoolwork. Many children

may cry or go off by themselves or even hurt themselves.

Grown-ups can help children **TAME**

TRAUMA BEASTIES. Children and grown-ups can

work together so that everyone will know when a

TRAUMA BEASTIE is pestering or

bothering them.

Grown-ups can hold children and

hug children to let them know they are

safe.

Grown-ups can remind children that they are only being bothered or pestered by a **TRAUMA BEASTIE**.

Children and grown-ups can both say loudly:

" GO AWAY, **TRAUMA BEASTIE**!! I AM SAFE! DO NOT BOTHER ME!!" "GO AWAY!! I AM SAFE!!"

Talking about the **TRAUMA BEASTIE** makes the

TRAUMA BEASTIE become

SMALLER

and SMALLER

and SMALLER

Until it DISAPPEARS ...

"ʕʕʕʕ *poof* ʕʕʕʕ"

Children can stop **TRAUMA BEASTIES** from pestering them by thinking of special things that make them go away.

Some children have trouble closing their eyes and thinking or imagining ways to stop **TRAUMA BEASTIES**.

But it can be easy when you know the tricks and practice them. LET'S TRY!

First, take a finger  and draw a **door** on your hand.

Next, close your eyes and draw the

door again. Remember, do it this time

with your eyes closed.

Now open your eyes. Think about

the **door**.

Finally, close your eyes and IMAGINE the **door**. Tell

your grownup what it looks like. What kind of doorknob it

has. If you cannot think and see the door with your eyes

closed, practice these special steps. Keep practicing, and

you will learn the trick!

Pete can think of his special **DOOR CLOSED,** with a

LOCK and **a STOP SIGN** on it.

Whenever **TRAUMA BEASTIE** thoughts or feelings bother Pete, he can think of his special **DOOR**. He can push those **TRAUMA BEASTIE** thoughts right behind the **DOOR** and shut it tight with the **LOCK** on!

Children can stop scary **TRAUMA BEASTIE** dreams, too. They can lie in bed, hold on to a special stuffed animal or doll, and with their eyes closed, say out loud three times:

1. "I'm not going to have any scary **TRAUMA BEASTIE** dreams!"

2. "I'm not going to have any scary **TRAUMA BEASTIE** dreams!"

3. "I'm not going to have any scary **TRAUMA BEASTIE** dreams!"

Susie is ready to go to sleep. She does not want scary

TRAUMA BEASTIE dreams. Susie closes her eyes,

holds onto her teddy bear and says out loud, in a strong

voice, **three times**, "I am not going to have any scary

TRAUMA BEASTIE dreams!"

I am not going to have any scary
TRAUMA BEASTIE dreams!
I am not going to have any scary
TRAUMA BEASTIE dreams!
I am not going to have any scary
TRAUMA BEASTIE dreams!

There is another way that children can keep **TRAUMA**

BEASTIES from tricking and bothering them.

Children can touch or tap special spots on their

bodies. These special tapping spots are energy spots. Your

body has energy around and in it. The tapping spots are

called acupressure points. This is a big and unusual word,

but it is an important word.

Tapping these special spots and saying special

words can help children feel brave, calm, courageous and

safe. Tapping moves out the **TRAUMA BEASTIE**

feelings and thoughts and moves in feelings, thoughts and

behaviors that will help you to be happy and to solve your

problems in a helpful way.

BUT there are two very important things to remember. While you are tapping, think and feel what you are tapping about. And remember that sometimes you have to do your tapping on your special statement more than once to really **TAME TRAUMA BEASTIE** feelings and thoughts.

The children in this book will show you each of the tapping points. Ready? Let's start!

We always start out rubbing the "tender spots." The tender spots are found about 2 or 3 inches down from our collarbone and about 2 or 3 inches out from the center. When these spots are rubbed, they can feel tender. That is why they are called tender spots! Pretty neat, huh!

Maria is rubbing her
tender spots.

After the tender spots are rubbed, two fingers, the

pointing finger and the middle finger, are used to tap the

special acupressure spots. Use the fingers on the hand you

color or write with.

Johnnie is tapping the first point at
the beginning of the eyebrow near
the nose.

Jane is tapping on the next point at
the side of her eye.

Andy is tapping on the point under his eye.

Jamie is tapping on the point under his nose.

Lizzie is tapping on the point at the hollow of her chin.

Jamal is tapping on the point just under the start of his collarbone.

Luke is tapping on the point in the middle of his side, under his arm.

Jake is tapping on the last spot we use, called the "karate chop" point. This spot is on the side of the hand below the little finger or pinky.

Now you know all the special tapping spots, so let's learn how to use them.

A cool way to use the tapping spots is to do CHOICES. CHOICES not only helps you calm down but it helps you remember how to solve your problem.

To start CHOICES, you have to think of a special statement to help you **TAME TRAUMA BEASTIES**.

A special statement needs to be thought about carefully because it is YOUR statement. When you put it together, it says what your problem feelings are, and then it says how you will get rid of your problem feelings and feel better.

Remember Sally? She was feeling scared during her bath. The special statement Sally thought of is, "Even though a **TRAUMA BEASTIE** makes me scared, I choose to find it very, very easy to feel safe in my bath."

First Sally rubs her tender spots and says her special statement 3 times.

1. "Even though a **TRAUMA BEASTIE** makes me scared, I choose to find it very, very easy to feel safe in my bath."

2. "Even though a **TRAUMA BEASTIE** makes me scared, I choose to find it very, very easy to feel safe in my bath."

3. "Even though a **TRAUMA BEASTIE** makes me scared, I choose to find it very, very easy to feel safe in my bath."

Next, she taps on each energy spot several times while saying the first part of her special statement.

(start of eyebrow) **"TRAUMA BEASTIE** makes me scared."

(side of eye) **"TRAUMA BEASTIE** makes me scared."

(under eye) **"TRAUMA BEASTIE** makes me scared."

(under nose) **"TRAUMA BEASTIE** makes me scared."

(hollow of chin) **"TRAUMA BEASTIE** makes me scared."

(start of collarbone) "**TRAUMA BEASTIE** makes me scared."

(side/under arm) "**TRAUMA BEASTIE** makes me scared."

(karate chop) "**TRAUMA BEASTIE** makes me scared."

Sally now taps some more, and while she taps she says the **entire** second part of her statement.

(start of eyebrow) "I choose to find it very, very easy to feel safe in my bath."

(side of eye) "I choose to find it very, very easy to feel safe in my bath."

(under eye) "I choose to find it very, very easy to feel safe in my bath."

(under nose) "I choose to find it very, very easy to feel safe in my bath."

(hollow of chin) "I choose to find it very, very easy to feel safe in my bath."

(start of collarbone) "I choose to find i very, very easy to feel safe in my bath."

(side/under arm) "I choose to find it very, very easy to feel safe in my bath."

(karate chop) "I choose to find it very, very easy to feel safe in my bath."

Finally Sally taps and switches between the beginning and ending of her special statement. Look how she does this.

(start of eyebrow) "**TRAUMA BEASTIE** makes me scared."

(side of eye) "I choose to find it very, very easy to feel safe in my bath."

(under eye) "**TRAUMA BEASTIE** makes me scared."

(under nose) "I choose to find it very, very easy to feel safe in my bath."

(hollow of chin) "**TRAUMA BEASTIE** makes me scared."

(start of collarbone) "I choose to find it very, very easy to feel safe in my bath."

(side/under arm) "**TRAUMA BEASTIE** makes me scared."

(karate chop) "I choose to find it very, very easy to feel safe in my bath."

Now Sally is finished doing Choices, and she feels relaxed. She takes a deep breath and enjoys her bath.

John became scared while playing tag. His special statement is, "Even though a **TRAUMA BEASTIE** confused and frightened me, I choose to find it very, very easy to feel safe playing tag with my friend."

First John rubs his tender spots and says his special statement 3 times.

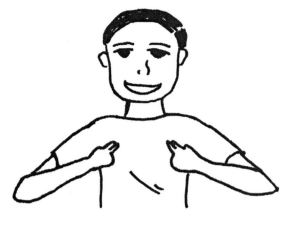

1. "Even though a **TRAUMA BEASTIE** confused and frightened me, I choose to find it very, very easy to feel safe playing tag with my friend."

2. "Even though a **TRAUMA BEASTIE** confused and frightened me, I choose to find it very, very easy to feel safe playing tag with my friend."

3. "Even though a **TRAUMA BEASTIE** confused and frightened me, I choose to find it very, very easy to feel safe playing tag with my friend."

Next, he taps on the energy spots and says the first part of his special statement.

(start of eyebrow) **"TRAUMA BEASTIE** confused and frightened me."

(side of eye) **"TRAUMA BEASTIE** confused and frightened me."

(under eye) **"TRAUMA BEASTIE** confused and frightened me."

(under nose) **"TRAUMA BEASTIE** confused and frightened me."

(hollow of chin) **"TRAUMA BEASTIE** confused and frightened me."

(start of collarbone) **"TRAUMA BEASTIE** confused and frightened me."

(side/under arm) "**TRAUMA BEASTIE** confused and frightened me."

(karate chop) "**TRAUMA BEASTIE** confused and frightened me."

Now John taps and says the entire second part of his statement.

(start of eyebrow) "I choose to find it very, very easy to feel safe playing tag with my friend."

(side of eye) "I choose to find it very, very easy to feel safe playing tag with my friend."

(under eye) "I choose to find it very, very easy to feel safe playing tag with my friend."

(under nose) "I choose to find it very, very easy to feel safe playing tag with my friend."

(hollow of chin) "I choose to find it very, very easy to feel safe playing tag with my friend."

(start of collarbone) "I choose to find it very, very easy to feel safe playing tag with my friend."

(side/under arm) "I choose to find it very, very easy to feel safe playing tag with my friend."

(karate chop) "I choose to find it very, very easy to feel safe playing tag with my friend."

Finally John taps and switches between the beginning and ending of his special statement.

(start of eyebrow) "**TRAUMA BEASTIE** confused and frightened me."

(side of eye) "I choose to find it very, very easy to feel safe playing tag with my friend."

(under eye) **"TRAUMA BEASTIE** confused and frightened me."

(under nose) "I choose to find it very, very easy to feel safe playing tag with my friend."

(hollow of chin) **"TRAUMA BEASTIE** confused and frightened me."

(start of collarbone) "I choose to find it very, very easy to feel safe playing tag with my friend."

(side/under arm) "**TRAUMA BEASTIE** confused and frightened me."

(karate chop) "I choose to find it very, very easy to feel safe playing tag with my friend."

John takes a deep breath, laughs and runs after his friend.

Maria was asleep but woke up scared. Her special statement is, "Even though a **TRAUMA BEASTIE** woke me and frightened me, I choose to find it very, very easy to remember I am safe and my mother is safe and I can go back to sleep."

First Maria rubs her tender spots and says her special statement 3 times.

1. "Even though a **TRAUMA BEASTIE** woke me and frightened me, I choose to find it very, very easy to remember I am safe and my mother is safe and I can go back to sleep."

2. "Even though a **TRAUMA BEASTIE** woke me and frightened me, I choose to find it very, very easy to remember I am safe and my mother is safe and I can go back to sleep."

3. "Even though a **TRAUMA BEASTIE** woke me and frightened me, I choose to find it very, very easy to remember I am safe and my mother is safe and I can go back to sleep."

Next, she taps on the energy spots and says the first part of her special statement.

(start of eyebrow) "**TRAUMA BEASTIE** woke and frightened me."

(side of eye) **"TRAUMA BEASTI**
woke and frightened me."

(under eye) **"TRAUMA BEASTIE**
woke and frightened me."

(under nose) **"TRAUMA BEASTIE**
woke and frightened me."

(hollow of chin) "**TRAUMA BEASTIE** woke and frightened me."

(start of collarbone) "**TRAUMA BEASTIE** woke and frightened me."

(side/under arm) "**TRAUMA BEASTIE** woke and frightened me."

(karate chop) "**TRAUMA BEASTIE** woke and frightened me."

Marie now taps and says the entire second part of her statement.

(start of eyebrow) I choose to find it very, very easy to remember I am safe and my mother is safe and I can go back to sleep.'

(side of eye) I choose to find it very, very easy to remember I am safe and my mother is safe and I can go back to sleep."

(under eye) I choose to find it very, very easy to remember I am safe and my mother is safe and I can go back to sleep."

(under nose) "I choose to find it very, very easy to remember I am safe and my mother is safe and I can go back to sleep."

(hollow of chin) "I choose to find it very, very easy to remember I am safe and my mother is safe and I can go back to sleep."

(start of collarbone) "I choose to find it very, very easy to remember I am safe and my mother is safe and I can go back to sleep."

(side/under arm) "I choose to find it very, very easy to remember I am safe and my mother is safe and I can go back to sleep."

(karate chop) "I choose to find it very, very easy to remember I am safe and my mother is safe and I can go back to sleep."

Finally Maria taps and switches between the beginning and ending of her special statement.

(start of eyebrow) "**TRAUMA BEASTIE** woke and frightened me."

(side of eye) "I choose to find it very, very easy to remember I am safe and my mother is safe and I can go back to sleep."

(under eye) "**TRAUMA BEASTIE** woke and frightened me."

(under nose) "I choose to find it very, very easy to remember I am safe and my mother is safe and I can go back to sleep."

(hollow of chin) "**TRAUMA BEASTIE** woke and frightened me."

(start of collarbone) "I choose to find it very, very easy to remember I am safe and my mother is safe and I can go back to sleep."

(side/under arm) "**TRAUMA BEASTIE** woke and frightened me."

(karate chop) "I choose to find it very, very easy to remember I am safe and my mother is safe and I can go back to sleep."

Maria takes a deep breath and goes back to sleep.

It took courage to read *Taming Trauma Beasties*. Good for you! All of us are proud of you.

You are now a **TAMER** of **TRAUMA BEASTIES**. Even though really, really scary or hurtful things have happened to you, you are a GREAT KID. You now have the tools you need to stop **TRAUMA BEASTIES** from tricking, bothering and pestering you.

The End

Appendix A: Additional Examples for Therapists, Parents, and Caregivers

It is possible to focus not only on specific situations with Choices but also pervasive feelings, beliefs and attitudes. The child can develop a working phrase and tap on it each day. Included here are examples of such phrases. Each example described below is drawn from actual cases, sometimes from a number of cases combined into one.

Zack is a 10-year-old boy who witnessed his father beating his mother. He refused to talk in therapy about these memories despite his severe generalized anxiety. He was taught the Trauma Beastie concept as a way to contain traumatic thoughts, feelings and behaviors. He was especially interested in the idea that a Trauma Beastie can pester and bother you, causing you to worry and to feel scared and anxious. Zack agreed to develop a special statement, "Even though I am worried about being bothered by a TRAUMA BEASTIE, I choose to find it very, very easy to be brave and remember I am safe." It was decided that he needed to perform Choices three times a day: when he woke up, when he got home from school, and before he went to bed. This procedure was followed for two months, and during that time he slowly became able to acknowledge his father's violent behavior.

Jill, age 8, suffered severe neglect and was placed in foster care at age 5. Her sense of deprivation was so profound that she would go into the other family members' closets and count the number of shirts and jeans each child had. She would become verbally and even somewhat physically aggressive whenever she was told "no." The Trauma Beastie concept was explained to her and to her foster mother. Because of her need to feel special, it was decided that Jill would do Choices with her foster mother. When she was finished, they would have a special activity together, such as a snack, a game or a story. The morning was too hectic for the foster mother, so Choices was done after school and before bed. Jill's special statement was, "Even though a TRAUMA BEASTIE confuses me and I get angry when my foster mom says no, I choose to find it very, very easy to remain calm and remember that 'no' is loving and safe." Jill was able to respond appropriately to "no" after only 2 weeks of this new regimen.

Tommy was afraid to sleep in his bedroom. He became hysterical and physically aggressive if forced to sleep there. His parents could not identify a reason for his fear but reported that it had been going on for three months. He had been sleeping in the computer room with all the lights on. When his parents fell asleep, he went into the hall and put those lights on as well. Rewarding him for sleeping in his room had not worked, because he waited until his parents fell asleep and then left his room and went to the computer room. Talking with Tommy revealed that he was brave in many other situations. The therapist praised him and told him about Choices. Tommy was told that his bravery in riding horses could be used to help him sleep in his own room. A working phrase to help him apply his resources to his fear of sleeping in his room was,

"Even though I am scared to sleep in my bedroom, I choose to find it very, very easy to be as brave in my bedroom as I am riding horses." Tommy tapped, lying on his bed, in the morning and after school. After three days, he was able to sleep in his bedroom with only a nightlight.

Jessy, age 4, had open-heart surgery at 8 months of age, and the tip of her thumb was accidentally cut during preparation for discharge. At one moment, she was happily sitting on her mother's lap, and the next she was screaming and being rushed to surgery for stitches. This trauma later manifested as a severe startle response. Jessy became easily startled by any unexpected sound and would become still and stare off into space. She avoided active peer play. It was decided that her mother would tap for her and, during the tapping, Jessy could participate as she wished. The working phrase was, "Even though I get easily scared by surprised loud noises, I choose to find it very, very easy to keep breathing and remember I am safe." Jessy and her mother tapped each evening before Jessy went to sleep. Her mother reported a slow and steady decline of the startle response over the next month.

Bryan, age 9, was born with one kidney and was stabilized but in renal failure. He was very fearful that he would need a kidney transplant and was experiencing separation anxiety and generalized anxiety. He also resented the fact that he had to be on a special diet that restricted his favorite foods, such as ice cream and pizza, and that he had to take many pills. Bryan agreed to do Choices every day after school. His working phrase was "Even though I worry about my kidney not working and needing surgery, I choose to find it very, very easy to remain brave, eat the right things and take my pills." Although Bryan's condition has continued to be fragile, his utilization of Choices has led to absolute compliance to medical dictates and continued stabilization.

Summary

Trauma comes in all sizes, forms, and levels of intensity. A working phrase can be developed to help a child get back on a bike after a nasty fall as well as for a child who has suffered severe abuse. Scary and painful things happen to children all over the world. As mental health professionals, parents, guardians, and foster parents, we can give children the tools to heal and to alter their lives in profound ways. Trauma is like a crippling disease that infects relationships, schools, workplaces, cities and countries. Choices is one way to stop the devastating impact of trauma and truly heal the children of the world. The stories described in this book are only a few of the countless examples that could have been given.

Additional resources are listed in the next appendix.

Appendix B: Resources

Association for Comprehensive Energy Psychology, www.energypsych.org.

Carrington, P. (2001) *How to create positive choices in energy psychology: The choices training manual.* Kendall Park, NJ: Pace Educational systems.

Craig, G. (1999) *Emotional freedom techniques: The manual (3rd ed).* El Paso: Mediacopy. Also available at www.emofree.com.

Yordy, J. (2006) Children and teens: Using magic fingers to energize youngsters. In R. Ball (Ed.), *Freedom at your fingertips: Get rapid physical and emotional relief with the breakthrough system of tapping.* Fredericksburg, VA: Inroads Publishing.

Other books about trauma/psychology from ThomasMax:

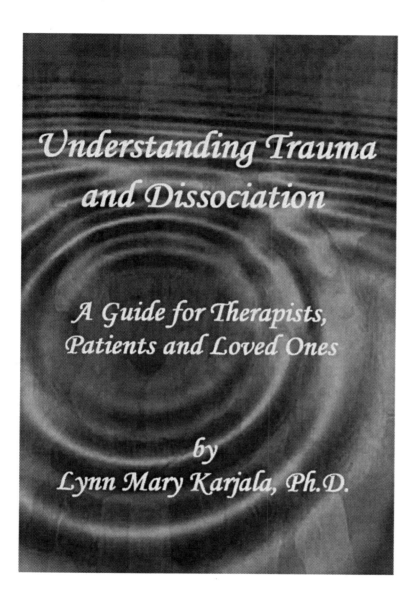

Dr. Karjala's book is available through her website, karjala.com, as well as through bookstores and internet merchants.

Understanding Trauma and Dissociation, a Guide for Therapists, Patients and Loved Ones by Lynn Mary Karjala, Ph.D., $ 14.95

Dr. Karjala, co-author of **Taming Trauma Beasties**, breaks down unravels the mystery of dissociation in this "must-read" book for psychotherapists who treat the aftereffects of trauma, as well as for trauma survivors and their loved ones. In simple and clear language she explains the connection between dissociation, trauma, and the devastating physical and psychological symptoms that stem from them. She offers a thorough description and understanding of the three phases of trauma treatment with an eminently practical guide for using the Quintessential Safe Place to minimize the terrifying experience of retraumatization by the flooding of traumatic feelings and thoughts. There is an engaging description of the "critical voice/protectors," a very active internal system aimed, among other things, at derailing treatment and preventing the patient from experiencing any hope of recovery. Finally, there is an introduction to mind-body techniques and their application to the treatment of trauma.

Other books for young readers from ThomasMax:

IncrediBoy: Be Careful What You Wish by Lee Clevenger, $ 12.95

To Christian Savage, age 11, life is a cruel joke. He's the smallest kid in his class, unpopular and a target for bullies. Worse, his older brother is "Mr. Perfect Boy," a star athlete and student to whom Christian is always being compared. To escape life's cruelties, Christian resorts to daydreams, and in his favorite fantasy, he's a superhero he calls *IncrediBoy*. His life changes when he finds two rings lost by Yoqe, an evil man-eating alien, and through the magic of the rings, he becomes *IncrediBoy* in real life. But Christian quickly learns that being a superhero isn't all it's cracked up to be. And Christian doesn't know it, but Yoqe is on his way back to Earth to reclaim his rings. Can Christian's incredipowers defeat Yoqe? Or will Christian be the alien's next meal? Or could it be Christian has an un-incredible ace up his sleeve for his showdown with Yoqe? For ages 9 and up, includes "incrediglossary" to help young readers with words they might not recognize such as "oxymoron" and "perpetual" and, of course, "incrediwords" like "incredispeed."

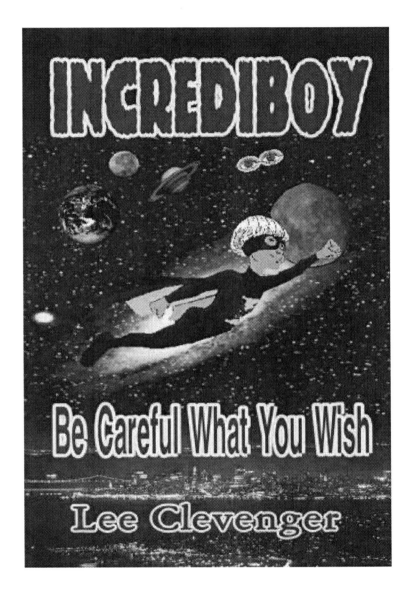

All **ThomasMax** books are available at stores wherever new books are sold. If the book you want is not in stock, ask the store to order it for you. Or you can buy **ThomasMax** books from internet sellers such as Amazon.com or Barnes and Noble (barnesandnoble.com). You may also order any **ThomasMax** book from the thomasmax.com website via PayPal account.

LaVergne, TN USA
05 May 2010
181565LV00001B/68/A